THE CORRS

THE CORRS

THE AUTHORIZED BEHIND-THE-SCENES BOOK
CORNER TO CORNER · PAUL GASTER

ANDRE DEUTSCH

First published in Great Britain in 1999
By André Deutsch Limited
76 Dean Street
W1V 5HA
www.vci. co.uk

Text, photography and design copyright © Paul Gaster, 1999

A catalogue record for this book is available from the British Library.

ISBN 0 233 99634 6

Printed and bound in the UK
by Jarrold Book Printing

1 3 5 7 9 10 8 6 4 2

CORNER
TO
CORNER

introduction

The Corrs' manager, John Hughes, reckons that 'a photographer is about as welcome as sand in your eye'. You can still manage to function if you have to but it's really annoying. It's just as annoying if you're the sand.

Seven years and thousands of photographs on since I'd first started shooting an unknown band from Dundalk, Ireland, I was standing on stage waiting for The Corrs to make their entrance for the biggest concert of their lives. A sell-out headline stadium concert in front of 42,000 people, all of whom had come to see just one thing, The Corrs. What's more, it was in Dublin, and a homecoming to end all homecomings. There would be other stadium concerts but this moment would always be unique.

All I could think was 'I hope to God I get some good shots', because there wouldn't be a second chance. The whole of the book depended on the next two hours.

I'd done as much as I could in advance, checked out the best vantage points, but the Lansdowne Road stadium, home of Irish rugby, had been empty then. From my position at the side of the stage I couldn't see a thing except the back of the curtain, but I knew that by now there wouldn't be an inch of ground uncovered. And I knew I would have to climb over practically every part of the stadium, fighting through fans and security, in an effort to capture the event.

The intro music ended, the curtains opened and there they were: 42,000 expectant, upturned faces. All you could see were people. 'Wow,' I kept saying to myself, 'wow, I should have been a musician.'

The daunting view from the stage of the empty stadium during sound check the afternoon before the Lansdowne Road show.

first contact

This whole book happened by accident. After spending four years at college studying business and economics, two topics I don't wish to hear about ever again, I decided what I really wanted to be was a film director. For Christmas one year my parents had bought me a camera, very generous of them but hardly state of the art having been made in communist East Germany. My plan was to use it to learn about light, something I thought that film directors had to understand before they were let loose on actors and a script.

So here I was in 1992 with no job but an old Cold War single lens reflex camera, learning about light through the revolutionary approach of photographing leaves and twigs, when I was volunteered to do a photo shoot with some band I'd never heard of. I'd just returned from teaching English in Spain and had come back with a few nice shots, but I'd never liked taking pictures of people. I'd found it very intrusive.

My father had been talking to an old friend, John Hughes, about a band John had just started to manage, when the topic of promotional photos had come up. Shots were needed

This shot from the first shoot best captures what I was after and gives an idea of what was to become the band's image.

One of the first shots I took of the girls while we were waiting for Jim to show up.

to accompany this band's demos which were soon to be sent off to the record companies. The most important thing about the photographer, John said, was that he must be cheap. My father, remembering that I had artistic pretensions and, more importantly, a camera, said with his usual self-confident exuberance, 'Paul will do that!' and I was hired.

To say that there was a budget would be to bestow on the project more credibility than it perhaps deserved. But at least I might learn something and experience was more important than money. So armed with camera, film and a fair amount of trepidation, I reported to Ardmore Film Studios for my first job as a professional photographer.

**Jim turned up and we got down to
work under the supervision of John Hughes,
The Corrs' manager.**

Ardmore Studios, in County Wicklow, is just a few miles south-east of Dublin. The band were appearing in a music video to promote a charity single. I can't now remember what the song was, or even the charity. But the lead vocal was sung by singer/songwriter Paul Brady and the video was being directed by none other than Jim Sheridan, director of *My Left Foot* and *In the Name of the Father*. Everybody was giving their services for free and The Corrs – or the girls at least – had managed to land the gig as backing singers both on the single and in the video. This was no mean feat for a group of complete unknowns.

But seven years down the road, it doesn't really surprise me. The Corrs' ability to seize an opportunity and capitalize on it has been a hallmark of their success. Many's the time I've heard them say, 'You never know what might come out of it, or who you might meet.' It's this approach that has got them where they are – not forgetting all the hard work.

I had been given an hour to do some shots before the girls were needed for the video. Having arrived a little early I'd done a scout around the studio's back-lot looking for a suitable location. To my delight I found an old set for the detective series *Remington Steel*, starring Pierce Brosnan. In one episode Remington Steele had gone to the South of France so the obvious and natural thing to do was to build the South of France in Ireland. I'd been asked to shoot the pictures in black and white and the crumbling brickwork and flaking plaster would provide texture and contrast, I thought, to the figures of The Corrs themselves. The seedy atmosphere of the place got my imagination going.

I was equally delighted when it came to meeting the band – or the three girls, as Jim hadn't yet showed. Not only because I'd just met three very pretty young women, but because I knew even then that it's much easier to make good-looking pictures with good-looking people.

So with much relief I set about explaining what I wanted to do. All three were eager to give it a go and as we started the shoot I began watching them react and interact, something I am still doing all these years later.

Three baby faces get briefed
by director Jim Sheridan.

That morning the whole business was as much a novelty for them as it was for me and they were understandably a touch nervous.

Andrea, at seventeen, took to it the quickest, turning on a coy, youthful flirtatious charm. It's a sort of ingenue quality that makes her easy to photograph, indeed sometimes it seems too easy and the shots don't always translate as well as they should.

Sharon, who was then twenty-two, was the most Irish-looking of the trio. With her high

In the backstreets of
Marseilles-style pimp shot.

cheek-bones and delicate features she had a touch of the Maureen O'Haras about her. Although she was obviously the oldest, taking the lead in asking questions and making small talk as big sisters do, her confidence didn't extend to feeling totally comfortable about being photographed. To some extent she needed cajoling and to be caught unaware to photograph well.

Finally there was Caroline, then aged nineteen. At first I thought she might be a problem; being the middle sister, I sensed, didn't suit her. Without the big-sister confidence of Sharon and the flirtatiousness of Andrea, she seemed a little unsure of herself, quiet and introverted. The other two, obviously used to this reticence, made an extra effort with her, encouraging her, fixing her hair and so on. Even so, until I developed the film I wasn't sure how the pictures would turn out. I needn't have worried as Caroline is one of those people the camera just loves. Sometimes it seems that you only have to point the camera at her to get a good shot.

What was beginning to concern me was that I was already thirty minutes into my allotted hour and Jim still hadn't showed. He was then twenty-eight, a working musician, and it seemed he had already acquired one of his profession's habits – being late. He turned up in the end and we got going.

The theme my imagination had conjured up was of a Mediterranean-style pimp with his prostitutes in some back street in Marseille. Their dark sultry looks and their image, which was remarkably fully formed for a band at such an early stage of their career, seemed ideally suited to it. Of course I didn't tell them about the theme – not entirely appropriate for a brother and three sisters after all – although I did venture to suggest that Jim used a flick-knife as a prop. John, their ever-watchful manager, quickly quashed that idea.

John Hughes had started out as a musician himself, and it's his knowledge of both music and the music business, combined with the closeness that exists between him and the band, that has created a special relationship. In France they would call him an *eminence grise*, a wise man who will never give you an answer until he's looked at the question from every possible angle, and sometimes not even then. It can be somewhat disconcerting to have him around while you're working, standing arms slightly folded, quietly watching. He never gives the game away about what he's thinking, except to point out that something's not right or to offer some words of encouragement to the band. They are his primary concern. Get in their way and you're history, no matter who you are. Some people speak softly and carry a big stick. That's John.

As the shoot went on they all relaxed and got more into it, putting up with my endless configurations and alterations. Sharon, move down a bit please; Caroline, could you look at the camera; Jim, could you take a pace to your right and turn your head to the left, over and over as I moved around them, focus, frame, click. Then, almost as soon as we'd begun, the

Andrea looks sultry as Sharon does her best Maureen O'Hara impression.

As you can see, I needn't have worried about how the shots of Caroline would turn out.

band were called for the video shoot. I stuck around, shooting whatever I could, trying to take advantage of the set lighting. In the video itself the girls had little to do except stand, mime along to their singing on the backing track and add a little glamour to the shoot.

Leaving the sound stage all six of us piled into John's car and headed off to Glendalough, the picturesque site of a sixth century monastic settlement, where the video continued and this time I took advantage of the daylight for another quite different set of photographs.

Three different contexts, and nine rolls of film. I felt elated. Totally confident. Or so I let them think. In fact, I had no idea how the shots would turn out. What I did know was that I had over-exposed half of the film by putting the camera to the wrong setting and I was convinced the rest would be out of focus or otherwise no good. With the help of a friend and a degree of luck I was able to rectify most of my technical mistakes and get myself out of gaol with a few good pictures. And that's all you need. It didn't take me very long to learn that film is the cheapest part of the procedure and you have to have the courage to make mistakes.

Looking back at those photographs now it's fascinating to see how The Corrs have changed and yet how, in some ways, they haven't changed at all.

Although this was at the very beginning of their career, the main ingredients were already in place: their looks, their image, their attitude and their drive. They might not have been as self-assured and polished as they are now, but even though I'd never heard any of their music or seen them play, they left an impression on me that day, an impression confirmed when I developed what I had shot. In spite of my novice status and lack of technical proficiency, the prints that emerged from the trays of chemicals had something, something that gave me a quiet satisfaction.

showcase

I didn't meet up with The Corrs again for about a year. They'd gone home to Dundalk, a small border town in County Louth, about halfway between Dublin and Belfast. I'd heard through my father, who had a management company and was by now their agent, that they were busy writing their own songs.

What sort of music they were working on I didn't know, as I still hadn't heard them play. Nobody had. Andrea was still at school, so there could be no question of touring. It was the classic Catch 22 situation. If you don't play no one will get to hear you. If no one hears you, you won't get any offers to play.

John Hughes knew that he had to set up a gig in Dublin to have any chance of getting a record company interested. As the band were still complete unknowns who had never played a real live gig, had never released a record and didn't have any fans, it was difficult for them to find a venue. But my father knew the owner of a club called The Waterfront, who agreed to let them play there. In fact, it was at this very club that the band had auditioned a couple of years earlier for *The Commitments*.

With the venue found there was one more obstacle to overcome – filling the club with enthusiastic supporters, which they had to do if they wanted to persuade a record company that they were worth signing.

My favourite shot from the first gig. I feel it captures something of the mix in the band's music.

This is what the gig was
actually like.

Friends and relations were bussed down from Dundalk while anybody who knew anybody who was even remotely famous was instructed to invite them. I was ordered to attend the occasion – along with everybody I knew – and under pain of death we were told that we had to enjoy ourselves. We all did our duty, roaring, shouting, screaming, demanding encores, but it was in vain. The record companies hadn't showed.

John had been in the music business long enough to know all about not giving up. The roaring, screaming and demanding of encores hadn't sounded like a put-up job to him. And the feedback was good. So renewed vigour was applied to the showcase idea and the usual suspects were rounded up once more. This time I was given the additional task of documenting the event. My budget again was fixed to the bare minimum, though this time my equipment was augmented with a flash my brother had got by collecting petrol tokens from our local garage.

The lights went out and the band came on stage. Only then did I realize that I could no longer see the meter in my very basic manual camera. Without a light reading, I couldn't set aperture or shutter speed. But I had no time to worry about little technicalities like that. The music began, the stage lights started to flash and the little needle inside my camera that gave light readings started to shoot up and down in time to the beat. I was now in the land of hit and miss with nothing to do other than start taking pictures, sometimes with flash, sometimes without. At least I was shooting in black and white, which is more forgiving than colour and allows for a wide margin of error.

The crowd was right up to the edge of the stage, giving it loads. I found the prospect of muscling my way up to the front to take photos a bit daunting at first. But as the audience was composed almost entirely of friends and relatives everybody was very obliging.

I had no idea what to expect or how I was going to photograph the gig. I just tried as many different approaches as I could think of, hoping for the best. Yet looking at the pictures now, it's funny to see that the interesting ones are not the ones used then – the shots that glamorize them – but the ones that show the reality. Not as sharp as they should be and too grainy, they're like The

Crowded and cramped, the girls do their awful and soon-to-be-defunct dance routine.

Corrs as they were then, a bit raw, a bit unfocussed but totally honest.

The band started somewhat tentatively, a little unsure of themselves. Gradually they moved up the gears, as the friendly audience, who knew what was at stake, roared their approval. With little experience and not much room to move as the stage was the size of an average front room, Andrea held onto the mike stand, half as support, half as psychological protection from the crowd. Now and then I saw her recognize a face or the sound of a voice and send a shy half coy smile in their direction. I could sense her being visibly lifted by the support of friends in the audience.

Jim, with years of experience on stage, seemed to settle the easiest, playing synth and guitar and exchanging smiles of encouragement with the others as they got into each new song. Sharon seemed absorbed in what she was doing, perhaps drawing on her own experience of playing in a classical orchestra.

Moody and dynamic,
these are the images that were
used as promotional shots.

Caroline, who was yet to take up the drums, played keyboards. Obviously still very shy, she seemed almost reluctant to peer out from behind them but as the evening wore on you could see her confidence grow and sense her enjoyment.

Partisan though they were, the crowd was impressed and by the end of the gig they were truly enjoying themselves. You could feel that kind of 'they're friends of mine, you know' vibe going around the room as people moved to the music. Once again, however, the people for whom all this had all been laid on, the record companies, hadn't showed.

Disappointed but undeterred, John decided to try one more time. Two 'sell-out' gigs at the Waterfront had brought their own momentum and the new venue was to be another Dublin club, Whelan's. New publicity material was needed, including a poster to promote the show.

This time it was to be a studio shoot – the first I'd ever done. Fortunately it was also a first for The Corrs, and as they didn't have much idea of what to expect my navigating in the dark wasn't too obvious.

And dark was the word. The brief was simple – four head shots and a group shot. They were dressed all in black and I decided to shoot them simply, framed by a black backcloth and enveloped in a black overcoat, which John wanted them all to wear. And so that's what they did, one at a time. For the group shot only one got to wear it – Sharon. Group shots are always difficult, even on the basic level of capturing everyone with their eyes open at the same time. It was important to avoid the all in one line, firing-squad approach. Overall it seemed to work. At least, their parents were pleased. They said I'd succeeded in capturing the personality of each of their offspring. I wasn't sure whether to be glad of this or not. I was just glad that the shoot had worked. Later I discovered that John had just been giving me a chance. If it worked, it worked, if it didn't, it didn't matter. That's not how I thought about it at the time.

As I walked into Whelan's on the night of gig, the sight of my poster on the wall gave me a bit of a thrill, even though someone said that with the text it made The Corrs look like a country and western band. I decided not to take any notice. This time I was back in my role of supporter and unhindered by cameras and worry, I could enjoy the proceedings, cheering and roaring with the rest of them.

It had been six months since the gig at The Waterfront and the band had obviously been working hard as both their sound and performance had improved. Once again the supporters' club gave their best and once again the important people, the record companies, didn't come.

But there was someone there who proved to be just as important, the American ambassador, Jean Kennedy Smith, sister of President Kennedy. She had come to the club as the guest of Bill Whelan, the musical brains behind *Riverdance*. So Impressed was she that she invited the band to play at the JFK library in Boston when America was hosting the soccer world cup in which Ireland was playing. As well as assorted congressmen and senators, including Ted Kennedy, the guests included the then Taoiseach, Albert Reynolds.

John had already been to the States and back several times on the band's behalf trying to get a record deal, but demo tapes and a few photographs were never going to have the same punch as the real thing. Jean Kennedy Smith's invitation meant all four of them could go and showcase their talent in person. Sadly – but not surprisingly – a photographer was not part of the deal. But a deal is what they came home with.

homecoming

As John Hughes never tires of saying, 'Getting a record deal is like being picked for the team – you haven't played a game, never mind won the cup.'

But, to continue the rugby analogy, being signed by Atlantic Records is like being selected by the All Blacks. After six months of recording sessions in Malibu, California, it was time to get off the bench and play. After a promotional tour in America The Corrs returned to Ireland. Their first album, *Forgiven, Not Forgotten*, was climbing the charts and a world tour was about to begin. They'd never have to rely on family and friends again.

Two years had passed since I'd last seen them. I had just returned from a spell working abroad and was determined to give photography a real try when I heard about the tour. It made sense that I should try to build on what I'd started. My father saw no reason why I shouldn't earn my keep and join the payroll of The Corrs' first Irish tour as an 'agent's representative' who happened to have a couple of cameras slung around his neck. After all, media interest was growing and that meant interviews and interviews needed pictures. As soon as I got the nod, I managed to sell the story to one of Ireland's glossy magazines. At least it would cover my film costs. John was at first a little worried, but I assured him I had no intention of abusing my position. The band would always have approval of any shots to be published, not that they have ever used their veto.

The tour bus was just that, a single-decker 30-seater white bus, with no mod cons and hardly spacious, especially as the band now included Anto Drennan on guitar and Keith Duffy on bass. It was a running joke that the world's two tallest musicians were playing with the world's most diminutive family band. Both Anto and Keith are about six foot five, but even with their matching long legs they somehow still managed to fit around the tiny tables on the bus.

Eight of the fourteen dates were already sold out, including the most prestigious at the National Stadium in Dublin. However, no one knew what the ticket situation was for the first gig, at the West County Hotel, Ennis, County Clare. During that 200-mile drive west from Dublin the atmosphere in

Not as sharp as I would have liked but this shot of Andrea was one of the first colour performance shots that really worked.

the bus was excited but tense. The Corrs had played to bigger audiences in the States while touring and promoting the album, but this was their first headline tour, the first time they had had to carry a show on their own.

When we reached our destination there was added excitement as we learned from the crew, who as usual had arrived there before us, that all 850 tickets for that night's gig were sold. But what kind of people would they be? No one had any idea of what constituted a Corrs audience, least of all The Corrs themselves. Would they be teenage girls identifying themselves with the sisters and cooing over Jim? Or would they be teenage boys ogling the sisters and envying Jim? Would they be an older crowd altogether, going for the sophistication of the band? The only thing for sure was that they weren't going to be heavy metalers.

The question appeared to be answered when the doors opened and a flood of teenage girls rushed excitedly to their places at the front. Along with them came some younger girls and boys accompanied by

mums, dads or older sisters. Then there followed the teenage boys, just as eager as their female peers but too self-conscious to show it. A little later the rest of the crowd started arriving. These were older, bunches of girls, girls and fellas mixed, young married couples, older couples with their families, 'trad' heads with their beards. Everybody.

But the real eye-opener for me that evening came from The Corrs themselves. I'd always admired what they did, but I hadn't seen them play since those early showcase gigs and though I'd been impressed by the album, a live performance can be very different. But neither I nor their CD-buying public would be disappointed. The sheer quality and professionalism of the band's performance was impressive. And as the tour went on and they grew in confidence, they got better still.

Andrea had blossomed as a performer. No more stuck-to-the-spot hugging of the mike. By the time we reached Dublin she was really moving, working every inch of the stage. Every gig seemed to free her more. The change was so pronounced that John was heard to say on several occasions that he hardly recognized her as the same girl who had set out with them three weeks earlier.

The exhilaration of touring was more than offset by the mundanity of the rest of tour duty. Time spent travelling in the bus was made easier with card games, *Blackadder* videos and regular stops at local shops for

munchies. Jim would be chatting while listening to his Walkman. Sharon would have her nose in a book, and not the airport variety. Once I saw her reading Albert Camus's *The Outsider*, which I had read when I was a student and hadn't liked because I thought it was too self-centred. She would have none of it. 'You've got to put it in its socio-historical context,' she remarked. 'Everyone had just gone through the war, having put their lives on the line for everone else. The idea of just living for themselves became very interesting.' And it wasn't pretentious, it was just what she thought. A bit like their music. Sometimes The Corrs are given stick for not being traditional enough. But the reason that the pop/rock edge they've given their music works, is because it's not contrived, it's just what they like and how they are.

On the bus I noticed a bit of playful rivalry between Andrea and Caroline, which was never in evidence when they were working. They're very close, with only a year between them. One of them had a thing about being tidy and got quite irked if the bus was a mess and the other would leave it untidy on purpose. The crew was there to iron out the hassles, but the band never took anyone for granted. They knew that no matter how late they had gone to bed or how early they had got up the crew had gone to bed later, drunk more and had had to get up hours earlier to make the next stop ready in time for the sound check.

With venues ranging from hotel function rooms, school halls and outdoor gigs the audiences in general ranged from 600 to 850. Getting the sound right was the number one priority and so once the crew had everything in place, the band would run through about half the set. The general sound in the venue would be perfected and any problems from the previous night's gig would be worked out, arrangements being changed if necessary.

The ritual rarely changed. Jim and Caroline would start on keyboards and drums, followed by Sharon on the

violin. Finally it would be Andrea's turn on lead vocal and tin whistle. They would continue the sound check until everything was right and if time was short would leave any minor worry until the following session.

Caroline had given up her keyboard role and in a little over a year had learned to play the drums and bodhrán, with the help of a teach-yourself video and her bodhrán teacher. Although all The Corrs had changed since I had seen them, it was most obvious in Caroline. She was totally transformed. Gone was the shy, retiring girl of two years before. She had been replaced by an ebullient young woman, full of fun and eager to laugh.

Mixed in with all the travelling, sound checking and performing were signings, interviews and television appearances. Everywhere they went someone wanted to talk to them, someone wanted them to sign something, someone wanted to touch them. Even in their hotel rooms they weren't safe. On one occasion, as Andrea was packing her bags to leave, a young chambermaid let herself into the room brandishing paper and pen. Andrea, though taken aback, signed but was a little disturbed by the incident and this feeling that she could be public property, even during private moments, was hard for her to come to terms with.

I was always surprised by how accommodating the band generally were. Each night following the gig they would arrange a room backstage for the fans. And, keeping up a steady flow of chat and banter, they would sign their records, posters or whatever other scraps of

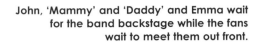

paper could be mustered, posing for photo after photo until every fan had been satisfied before making their way back to the hotel where, in theory, they were off duty. In practice they never were.

One night, in particular, a couple of guys exhausted the band's patience. With the next day off we were all having a few drinks in the hotel bar. The guys, with a few drinks taken themselves, wanted to be photographed with the girls. They started manhandling them into position, prodding and poking them while talking to each other as if the girls weren't there. Photos over, they invited themselves to the table and continued their curious behaviour much as before. The performance earned the pair a set of very chilly shoulders and they soon retreated. The respect The Corrs showed their fans wasn't always reciprocated.

After three weeks the tour was coming to a close with the final date at the Bantry Mussel Festival in County Cork. The festival, celebrating the local mussel harvest, runs over three days, attracting between six and nine thousand people a day to the town. The Corrs were the headline act on the final day.

We set off from Dublin early that morning to make sure of getting there on time. The road from Dublin to Cork City is a good one and the trip takes between two and four hours depending on who is driving. On the map Bantry only seems a short hop from Cork but with its twisty narrow roads the drive takes a good three hours.

The band had a signing to do in a record shop in Cork. With not enough time left for the drive to Bantry,

a helicopter was hired. The signing was going well, if running late, but the rush hour was just beginning. The motorcycle garda on duty told them not to worry and assured them he'd have them at the airport on time. True to his word, with the band barely on the bus and still waving goodbye, the garda put on his siren and flashing lights and took off. With a jolt the bus driver took off after him and just about stayed with him as he sped through the heavy traffic. Next it was out of the city and onto the two-lane airport road. Straight down the middle went the garda, waving maniacally to the traffic to clear a way. The band watched from the bus, now flat out in its effort to keep up, as cars and lorries swerved and whizzed past with what seemed like inches to spare. At the airport, still half-terrified, half-exhilarated, the band waved to their escort, boarded the helicopter and left the madness behind. They hadn't seen anything yet.

At Bantry the expected crowd of ten thousand had swelled to twenty. The place was Corrs mad. In our hotel, the lobby, the bar, the corridors were full of fans. As news arrived that the helicopter was landing the crowd legged it out the front to meet it, while the band slipped in the rear to the relative sanctuary of their rooms and a couple of hours of calm.

Respite over and it was into the cars and off to the town proper. The road in was lined with parked cars through which streamed columns of festival goers. Once in the town the mayhem was obvious with people milling around. As our cars passed people started to realize who they belonged to. At first they stared and pointed but as we neared the stage they started to crowd around, cheering in that eager drunken way that is the preferred mode of expression at three-day festivals. Near the stage some of the besieged security men had cleared a gap in the crowd and as the doors of the cars opened there was only one thing for it – leap out and run.

The crowd was overwhelming the organizers. Part of my job was working on the door, making sure people weren't getting in for free. That wasn't the problem here, it was safety. All I usually had to do was to make sure tickets were being checked, but this time I was press-ganged into the heavy stuff. The night before everybody on the tour had been give a leather jacket embossed with The Corrs' logo by the tour promoter as a souvenir known in the industry as 'swag'. These jackets now came in handy as security

One of the most difficult things about photographing a performance is the rapidly and constantly changing light. Judge it wrong and it's totally wrong, judge it right and it can be beautiful.

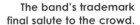

The band's trademark
final salute to the crowd.

uniforms. So looking as mean as possible, which is not very mean at all, I started my new career. My partner in this endeavour was Seanna, a gentle sort of bloke who had been driving us for the last three weeks. He did a much better impression of mean than me and so I felt we were safe enough.

My one regret in all the years I have spent photographing The Corrs is that I don't have one picture of that night. I'd been given the job of collecting the takings from the organizers, a surprisingly casual transaction, and had no alternative but to put the notes in my pocket. Thousands of pounds. So what with minding the money, watching that my cameras didn't disappear and lending a hand looking after the security of the band, photography wasn't an option.

The show was sheer craziness. Several times the band had to stop in an effort to persuade the crowd to move back for fear that someone at the front would be hurt. They would wait until the pressure was relieved and then, after a couple more songs, they would have to go through the whole thing again. With the gig – and several encores – played, and the crowd still baying for more, the

After the final show of the tour Andrea orchestrated these shots to let everybody see what The Corrs were 'really' like.

decision was taken to make a break for it. We rapidly ushered the band – and ourselves, too, for that matter – to the awaiting cars. From these cocoons we could see the pandemonium outside.

As we waited for our garda escort to clear a path through the throng, people were banging on the roof and the doors of our car, screaming and pressing their faces against the windows. I can only imagine what was happening to The Corrs in the car behind. At last a passage opened and heads down we set off. The driver of John's car had looked away at the wrong moment and before he could even get in gear it was swallowed back up by the crowd. Resigned to his fate, John got out of the car and waited the half an hour necessary for the crowd to disperse enough for him to leave.

It had been decided to stay in Cork rather than in Bantry and so back in the car park, a little away from the hotel entrance, the tour bus was ready. Not knowing what John was going through we waited. Crowds of people were roaming the hotel complex looking for the band. As rumour and counter-rumour spread we watched them run from the hotel lobby to the spot where the helicopter had landed earlier and back again, completely ignoring the little bus on the tarmac. When John turned up, the engine spluttered into life and the band slipped off into the night.

round two

I caught up with the band at regular intervals over the next couple of years. Sometimes I would have a commission from a magazine, sometimes I would turn up to get a different angle on the project I'd begun to plan and a couple of times I just went along for the free ride.

The first free ride was shortly after they had completed their tour of Ireland. They were playing a variety of venues and festivals around Europe, and had returned to Dublin to play at a rugby international between Ireland and the Barbarians in aid of the Northern Ireland peace process. The concert was at Lansdowne Road, venue of a future triumphal return that then couldn't have been much more than a dream. The stage, stuck in one corner, seemed tiny compared to the ominous vast space of the empty stadium but this didn't seem to rattle the band at all. Before they go on, they always seem very calm and together with no sign of nerves, but I have since learned that this is merely a very good front. You can tell how nervous they are by how quiet they are – the bigger the occasion, the quieter they become.

After the sound check there was the usual hanging around to be done. It was a beautiful sunny day and everybody naturally congregated on the steps in front of the organizers' building, close to the stadium. Tea and coffee were offered but it seemed beyond anyone's capability to organize biscuits until somebody had the bright idea of going to the gate and buying some off the street hawkers outside.

The advertising for the event hadn't been organized very well either, with the time The Corrs

Jim at The Factory rehearsal studios, Dublin, where the band rehearsed for a couple of weeks before their second world tour.

On the Denmark trip the entourage extended from Anto and Keith to a plane-full of fans.

were due to play not being the clearest. The result of this, along with the tradition of drinking that accompanies rugby internationals and the Irish tradition of always being late, was that in between a couple of under-15 mini rugby matches and the main event The Corrs played to a half-full stadium, the remainder of the crowd arriving in dribs and drabs. Seeming almost naked without the cover of darkness and the disguise of the light show, the band punched out a good half-hour set.

With the crowd still cheering it was into the bus and across the city to the airport – not quite the hectic journey across Cork but a race against time nonetheless – to catch a plane to Denmark and the open air Odense Festival. Odense is part of the European festival circuit that allows young bands to play to large and diverse audiences while guaranteeing them some earnings. Once through the boarding gates and onto the plane it was time to rest up before the next gig. Not likely.

The chartered plane was full of fans and the ladies and gentlemen of the press. The fans had won the chance to meet the band and fly with them to Denmark to see them play live. As the band went down the aisle to take their seats there was a big cheer and a round of applause. Once in the air and as 'refreshments' were distributed freely the band were off, making the rounds, chatting warmly to one and all before retaking their seats just as we arrived. It was then on to the festival, with our enlarged entourage being further lubricated along the way.

Compared to the drink being consumed by the revellers in Odense our crowd was only playing catch up, as the band could plainly see from backstage as they prepared to go on. The M.C. of the show must have been six foot five even without his big hair and platform shoes. Beside the girls he looked

Sharon clowns as she puts on her make-up backstage. The band says that performers, with their make-up and costumes, are all really just clowns deep down.

hilarious. From the crowd's reaction to his banter (in Danish) and his striptease, he seemed to be a pretty hilarious guy all round. As they came on he gave the band a big introduction, but even though their album had already gone double platinum in Denmark they had their work cut out for them. A large part of the audience had come to see the headline act, a Danish heavy metal band, and while most of the crowd were out to enjoy themselves there was a small element who seemed somewhat disaffected. A few of them even started to throw things but, undeterred, The Corrs launched into their set and whether the dissenters were silenced by security, by other members of the crowd or by the sheer quality of their performance, the band left the stage to an ovation.

However the day was far from over. The merry competition winners had been helping the even merrier members of the press keep up a fine tradition of their own. The flight home was, shall we say, very good-natured if thankfully quite short.

From Dublin the band flew off to resume their world tour which would last a year and a half from start to finish and would take them around the globe twice.

Ironically, their broad appeal was proving a minus rather than a plus when it came to building

Dublin by day

on their success on the road. The fact that their music didn't fit easily into any one category seemed to confuse the marketing people. It wasn't pop, it wasn't rock, it wasn't traditional, it wasn't folk, and they didn't see an obvious single on the band's album.

The introduction of Keith and Anto into the extended family had given the live sound more of a guitar orientation which the band would carry over into the second album, *Talk on Corners*, which was

Odense by night

released in October 1997.

Back in Dublin getting ready for the tour to promote the album's release, the band were at The Factory rehearsal studios for a couple of weeks before kicking off their second world tour at the Olympia Theatre. By the time I called by they were well into their second week and as I idled in I found Jim, Sharon and Caroline working on the arrangements for the new material.

Rehearsals and sound checks can be the most interesting part of the music business. Without the pressure of performance people play in a different way. They experiment more, mess about swapping songs. While most of the time it's pretty run of the mill, and even boring, every so often a small gem arrives with people playing for fun, just to enjoy each other. The playing might not have the energy of an on-stage live performance but sometimes the quieter moments can have a quality all their own. Away from the glamour, glitz and ego of the business, the musicians can revert back to the reason they got into music in the first place. Music itself.

I settled down in a chair to one side to watch the rehearsals and think about what I wanted to shoot. The atmosphere was relaxed and light-hearted with friends dropping in to say hi, people delivering stuff like a rake of violin bows for Sharon to try out or a selection of the band's newly discovered gadget, the mobile phone.

My own new gadget was a state of the art camera with low light lenses that would give the pictures better definition when not using a flash. I always prefer to use natural light and was eager to try them out. The sombrely lit rehearsal room was the perfect opportunity and I'd disturb nobody. Bit by bit I started to photograph the goings on.

It was now four years since the band's first gigs and they had a wealth of experience between them. It was clear to me that as individuals they had come more into their own and this in turn fed back into the music.

After lunch Andrea came in to work on lead vocal. As the day wore on she

This is a part of a magazine shoot I did on the siblings at Christmas. The shot would later get me into the Royal Albert Hall.

Andrea puts up the song list during rehearsals at The Factory.

found the room colder and colder, eventually donning a heavy woollen coat. Squatting precariously on the edge of her chair and sipping hot coffee she sang. All three girls squat peasant fashion from time to time and it can be quite disconcerting if one or more of them do it while you're talking to them as they practically disappear from view.

As they ended the set they arrived at one of their 'must do' songs, 'Runaway'. They began it as they'd done a million times before – until someone started hitting bum notes. The others took up the gauntlet and the whole thing was run through without a correct note in evidence. There wasn't a dry eye in the house as everybody broke up with laughter.

The time had come to put it all into practice: opening night at The Olympia. The two scheduled nights were sold out and they probably could have sold out a full week but with other commitments that was all the time they had. I was interested to see how some of the functions on my new camera would stand up to the test of a live show and had arranged to turn up and do some shots of the gig, again continuing what I'd been doing up to now. Or so I thought.

Arriving backstage my cosy world was somewhat disturbed when I heard the phrase 'the first three songs' directed not just at the other photographers milling around, but at me as well. It's a convention in the music business whereby the photographers covering a gig are herded into the pit in front of the stage and allowed to take photographs for the first three songs of the performance before been driven out of the auditorium. I had gone through this sometimes humiliating process once before while covering a three-day festival for a music magazine. I had basically spent three days

The business behind the performances. In most of the shots the band appear unaware of my presence but the shot of Sharon and Andrea shows a truer reflection of their attitude to the camera.

sitting outside the venue waiting for the first three songs of each act. So I decided I was never going to do that again.

There is a legitimate reason for this convention; it allows the press to get the shots they need, giving valuable exposure to the band, while preventing a media free for all. If you're a performer, having a photographer popping up and clicking away can destroy your concentration as surely as having somebody chatting in your ear. Video cameras, TV cameras, all those things get in the way, but some of them are necessary for the broader scheme, and some of them you can control, but some of them you just don't need. Like photographers. So they let the guys get their shots then they're out.

I know that every photographer and journalist thinks that they're different, that they would never abuse a trust, but I did feel I had some sort of relationship with the band and the next night I went back determined not to be in the same situation again.

I found John and told him of my predicament; how you can't really capture anything of the excitement and energy of a show by only photographing the beginning and how I couldn't even see Caroline from the pit. He relented, but added, 'What do you need all these pictures for anyway?' I'd been mulling over the same question myself for a while. I had tested the waters as a freelance both for the press and for picture agencies and had decided that what I really wanted to do was some long-term project work of my own. Most photographers dream of doing their own book and of being free from time restrictions, free from other people's agendas. 'I was thinking of doing a book,' I tentatively replied. 'Well,' he said in that exasperating way he has of giving a non-answer while he considers the idea, 'you'd certainly be the one to do it. You've got the pictures.' And with that he walked off.

All I can really remember about the gig that night is that though everybody seemed to be enjoying themselves, no one was having as good a time as I was. It might not have been a yes, but it wasn't a no. Even though the band hadn't seen much of my work, apart from a few magazine spreads from the first Irish tour, John had, and I knew he really liked it. So with even the possibility of such an opportunity in the air I roamed around the theatre, cameras at the ready (by now I had three) in a state of blissful excitement. And I carried on shooting right through to the encore.

The Corrs went off to Britain, returning for the Christmas break. As I still hadn't had anything like a definite answer from John, I started quietly lobbying. After a series of phone calls and postponed meetings I finally got the call to come over to discuss the idea. I had put together a portfolio of the mate-

Live at the Olympia, Dublin.
The first gig of the band's second world tour.

rial I had and brought this together with a formal proposal as to what I wanted to do (the first time my business studies course had come in useful). John seemed impressed by the proposal and definitely enjoyed looking back over the years of material he'd forgotten I had documented. When I left about an hour later he said that as far as he was concerned I had the commission but it would have to be okayed by the band.

The Corrs had been on the road for nearly two years and were about to embark on a promotional trip to Japan before heading south for their second tour of Australia and New Zealand, their first album having gone platinum nine times. I'd suggested to John that I went with them, but when departure day came they set off without me. So maybe that was it, I thought. Then a few days later I got a call, 'Come on out'.

It was now that I smacked into a wall of reality. How on earth was I going to pay for this? I tried to get an advance on the book, but there wasn't enough time. I did the proverbial begging, borrowing and stealing while the band agreed to front the costs of my travel and accommodation. On Wednesday night I got a call saying that my tickets would be couriered from London the next day, hopefully arriving by Friday evening in time for my flight on Saturday. They did and the following morning I was on my way to Sydney.

down under

It was now that I got my first introduction to life as an international pop star. My flight from Dublin, stopping over in London and again in Bangkok before arriving in Sydney, took the best part of twenty-four hours. The high point of the trip, apart from the eight spiffing films we were forced to watch, including *Mr Bean* twice, was the forty-five minute stop in Bangkok. I used this opportunity to stretch my legs and to be able to claim I'd been to Asia.

I can't sleep while on the move so here I was bang awake for the whole trip while everyone around tried to get some rest. I caused more than a little annoyance with my constant moving about and having my reading light on the entire time, a veritable beacon in the pervading gloom. You'd think I would have been exhausted after such an ordeal but no, by the time I was picked up at Sydney Airport at half past six on a stunningly sunny morning I was excited, wide-awake and eager to start work. The only problem was that everyone else was sound asleep in bed after the previous night's gig. With nothing else to occupy me, I decided to do the same. Big mistake. Half past six that evening and I was awoken by the phone. It was Emma, the Corrs' P.A. 'Hop in a cab and get down to the theatre.' She'd been trying to wake me since five.

I can only wonder at how the band does it. They'd been on the road for nearly two years. Planes, buses, cars and helicopters. Press conferences, hotel rooms, record shops and concert halls. I remember them telling me of one trip that went from Australia to Sweden, Sweden to America, America to Ireland, all within four days and with a gig to play at the end of each flight. And I thought the bus was bad.

Caroline at sound check.
As a band gets more popular the
venues, the stage and the drum kit
get bigger. The end result is that the
drummer becomes increasingly
difficult to photograph.

Down time in the green room backstage.

The family atmosphere is broken as Keith murders Jim.

John always used to say that no one would ever tour if they knew what it was like. But nobody does know what it's like until they've done it. Once you're on the road you're into a little routine and the routine keeps you going. You're hermetically sealed, shrink-wrapped. If you actually thought about what you were doing you'd come to a full stop.

I arrived at the State Theatre just after sound check. In the bowels of this beautiful marble-clad building the extended family had set up camp: band, crew, management, caterers, the full assemblage of thirty or forty people that it takes to put on a show. Down in the dressing rooms I nodded to the band who were getting ready for the gig. By now I was ravenous, so after saying my hellos I headed off to catering for sustenance.

With so many people on the road it becomes both convenient and economical to hire a team of caterers to tour with the band. I don't know how other bands operate but with The Corrs everyone, band and crew, eat the same food at more or less the same time. The band and the musicians tend to eat together, with the crew at a separate table. This is not a cast iron rule but just the natural result of the way each group lives and works. Just as the band and musicians become very close through constantly living and working together so do the crew, sharing rooms, flights, buses and time off. There is an overarching family atmosphere in the camp, an atmosphere

supported by the working ethos of the band as a whole. Indeed, many of the crew date back to that original 1996 tour of Ireland even though the band's popularity and the size of the show has grown.

Fed and watered, I set off to scout the theatre for the best locations and angles while getting some shots of the crowd coming in. As the lights went down I set myself up at the front of the stage, ready to start shooting. The band had been in Australia for a couple of weeks, and in Sydney for five days, so the local press had already covered the gigs and I had an open field, free from competition. The stage was quite low so I could get fairly close but I had to stay small and

Andrea is so physically expressive that she's great to photograph, while Caroline's face caught within the mass of drums and cymbals makes for more abstract shots.

move about a lot so as not to annoy anyone in the audience. I obviously didn't manage this as well as I thought, for after the show John said, half-joking, half-serious, 'Gaster, what's with all the front of stage business? I could hardly see for you in the way.' The rules of engagement when you're a photographer are unwritten and you only find them out as you break them. They also have a tendency to be rewritten as circumstances change. What might be fine on one occasion could be sacrilegious the next. You can only stay diplomatic. I was more careful next time.

The band got a rapturous reception from an already conquered crowd. The Corrs had once again upped the ante of their performance and now that they were well into this tour the tightness in their sound, a quality that they value so much, was more in evidence than ever. This tightness is akin to match fitness in sport when not only your body but also your mind is up to full speed.

You could tell that this Australian reception was special to them. Australia was the first place outside Ireland that they'd gone really big and there was a genuine warmth between

The band belt out the final strings of their encore before taking their by now customary end-of-show bow.

band and audience. The band seemed especially confident and sure of themselves here, working and relating to the audience with ease.

This was my first extended trip with The Corrs since 1996. I wanted to come to Australia as I had heard so much from Irish friends living there about how well the band was doing. They said that the place had gone Corrs mad. In every bar, shop, restaurant you went into you would hear the *Forgiven, Not Forgotten* album being played.

The tour was a sell-out and the atmosphere in the Corrs' camp was very relaxed. Gone was the giddy excitement of that first Irish tour. Now they were seasoned pros and there didn't seem to be much that could faze them. The band was still going through the necessary sound check routine but by now it was a far less structured affair. No longer was there a preordained order but for all that it was as professional as ever. It was just that by now everybody, band and crew, had their role off by heart.

Sound check is an odd time.
As the band run through their routine
they are at once working together
and completely alone.

The signing sessions and the interviews mean that the promotional grind never ends. I get an angry look from Andrea as I intrude on a moment's privacy.

Before the show, and sometimes after, there occurs the ubiquitous 'meet and greet' or, as the band refer to it on less optimistic evenings, the 'grip and grin'. This is their opportunity, showered and changed and ready for the show, to meet their fans, the competition winners, the local record company bigwigs and a range of assorted friends of friends, relations of relations. They value these gatherings, chances to meet the people who buy their records, to repay a debt of gratitude.

There are always people waiting around to see them both before and after the gig. Most times it's obvious why they're there: you can sense their excitement, you can see what it must mean to them. But there are others who make you wonder why they bothered, who treat the group as public property. The band, to their credit, always try to remain positive even in response to such questions as 'Which one are you?'

Later, when I asked Jim how he put up with it, his answer was, 'It's just part of the job.' Also, being a guy he finds it easier to be anonymous. Sharon is a natural at dealing with the press. So she often takes on the role of spokesperson. Avoiding the pitfalls of innuendo, she manages to be firm without insulting anybody or appearing too obstinate or opinionated. She can seem distant but it's only a defence mechanism against unwarranted familiarity, which is the one thing she

hates. But she is far from unfeeling. Her mantra is that everyone has to be respected. Once she was handed a letter by a fan at a signing that made her cry. The letter was about how 'Runaway' had given him and his wife strength when their baby was stillborn. 'I know what other people's music can do for me but it's hard to appreciate what ours does for other people,' she said, 'and it's something you really have to be aware of all the time, that it's not just a signature you're giving, it could mean the death of a child, or a love, a wedding, a funeral, it could be anything. That's why you have to give it the utmost respect.'

After each show the elation and the sweat is plainly obvious. Back in the dressing rooms The Corrs try to come down, try to let the crowd calm down and thin out. They try to be as open to the public as possible but sometimes there are too many people or they are simply not up to it and then it's a swift sprint off stage, no time to change, into the awaiting cars and back to the hotel. Even at their hotels they no longer have sanctuary. Jim, determined to enjoy himself, doesn't let other people deter him. Enjoying the company of the guys – musicians

Things had changed since the days of travelling around Ireland in a bus. Even so, when everything is organized for you, you are left totally in somebody else's hands.

and crew – he will find a quiet corner in the hotel bar for a couple of post-gig drinks. As is the nature of things, they sometimes hook up with other bands who happen to be touring at the same time and there will be much 'muso' talk for the rest of the evening. If there's even the remotest possibility of this happening I head for the hills.

The girls, on the other hand, have long since given up this small pleasure, preferring instead to get together in one of their rooms or to simply take a long, hot bath and unwind. Being in the public eye it is difficult for them to relax in such situations, except at home in Ireland with their friends. They used to enjoy the bars in the early days but by now the novelty of the after-show drinking session had worn off. They have seen the dependency

The band discuss the implications of the song list for an American album release. Everything is discussed and decided democratically with John.

that develops all too often amongst musicians, when the drink to help you come down after a show evolves into the only way it's possible to unwind. At other times they simply want to get away from it all and be alone for a while.

This desire to be out of the glare was one of the reasons I tried to be as inconspicuous as possible. This is very difficult when you're loaded down with cameras and trying to do your job. I'm never entirely at ease when doing reportage and sometimes when you sense someone's discomfort you just have to take the decision to put the cameras away. You just have to feel your way about.

Leaving Sydney, I got a sense of just how vast Australia is. Looking out of the window while driving to Newcastle, a couple of hundred miles north of Sydney, or fly-

The set-up for a show involves a lot of people and a lot of work. As the tour wears on any novelty that may remain wears off.

**Andrea takes some time away
from it all. Naturally
I have to disturb it.**

ing to Canberra, the land seemed to go on for ever and there didn't seem to be a soul living on it in between the cities. For that matter there didn't seem to be anyone living in Canberra either. We had been reliably informed that the population was over a quarter of a million but either they all lived in the only building to be seen, the parliament, or they were in hiding.

A local school was having an Irish day and had asked The Corrs to attend. I doubt whether they really expected The Corrs, the most popular band in Australia, to turn up, but they did. Sure enough as we came off the main road and headed towards the school, there were the houses and the people, hidden in amongst the trees. Everybody at the school, teachers and pupils alike, was very excited by the band's arrival. The school gym was full of kids in neatly packed rows of seats. After a dis-

play of Irish dancing by some of the students and an introduction by the Irish ambassador, The Corrs came on and said a few words before playing a short acoustic set. They hadn't much time before they had to head for that night's venue and sound check but they weren't allowed to leave until they did another song. Back in the classroom that had been set aside for them to get ready in there was much to-ing and fro-ing as posters, t-shirts and CDs were passed in for the band to sign by wide-eyed kids who stood outside the door.

From Canberra we set off for New Zealand via Sydney. I was in a considerable amount of discomfort after the two flights as almost miraculously I'd managed to pick up a head cold. I couldn't believe it. Getting ill on tour is one of the things the band fear most. They have a range

of potions, vitamins, supplements, painkillers, oils, remedies and old wives' cures for almost every ailment. I know this from the assortment of pills and mixes I was given when I told them of my predicament. Andrea, in particular, took an interest in my well-being, mixing and shaking up all sorts of combinations. I'm sure she would have had a few spells to cast if need arose.

In New Zealand they were to play in all three major cities: Christchurch, Wellington and Auckland. While their success here was not quite as phenomenal as in Australia their album had still gone to number one and all three venues had sold out. It appeared that everything here would be plain sailing. However, on our arrival Henry, the band's much-loved tour manager, was faced with a completely unforeseeable problem that jeopardized the Auckland gig.

Much to the country's acute embarrassment the major power lines into Auckland, New Zealand's biggest city, had become overloaded and blown up. What was worse was that it would be months before they could be replaced. It seemed doubtful that the gig would go on but, after a bit of crisis management on Henry's part, it was established that the emergency generator at the venue could cope with the power requirements of the show.

Although the antipodean tour was nearly over, there was no let up in the pressure. News had come in that The Corrs' new single in Germany, 'What Can I Do?', was about to break and a video was needed quickly. Also, up-to-date group photographs were needed for the new programme that would accompany the forthcoming UK tour. I was delighted as it gave me the opportunity to do a series of set-up shoots which otherwise I would have had a hard time per-

During one of the shows this little girl was allowed into the pit in front of the stage. It's almost as if she got a show all to herself.

**This is the last gig on the tour.
I knew the shot I wanted
and climbed up on the back
of some vacated chairs
to get the viewpoint.**

suading the band to agree to. Once in Christchurch I scouted some locations and the shoot was set up. I'm sure this wasn't a popular decision but as always when the band see something as being necessary, they turn up willingly.

Across the road from our hotel I'd found a great location – a derelict building that had been plastered over so it would not be too much of an eyesore. Through it ran a set of tram tracks that gave the place an interesting geometry that really caught my eye.

Most bands hate being photographed out of context. Standing around looking sultry or hunky is not what they do. They are musicians and usually it's only the front man who really has a feeling for how to project into the camera. The Corrs are no exception. I always try to be as diplomatic as possible, not favouring any particular member too much.

On the shoot we were chaperoned by Emma, but without an assistant to help load cameras and change lenses I was under a bit of pressure. I could tell that this wasn't exactly how the band had planned to spend their morning off with Jim, especially, moving about distractedly. The whole lot of us had to move a bit more rapidly and a little less distractedly every time a tram came through but I managed to get what I wanted. After a series of portraits it was on to the Town Hall, the next location. Here it was more of the same and once the shoot was over you could see the relief on the band's faces just before they scarpered. Looking back over the contact sheets I was horrified to see the faces on them, but in the end all you need is the one shot.

These are some of the shots taken for the ill-fated concert programme.

Backstage the band wait to
come on for their encore.
Encore done and it's straight
out and into the awaiting cars.

On the last day of the tour the girls went off on one of their favourite pastimes – shopping – while Jim went off somewhere to see some beach. I went down to a local musical shop with Keith and the rather cultured Conor Brady, the guitarist who was deputizing for Anto Drennan on this tour. (With some reluctance, the band had granted Anto a well-deserved sabbatical to tour with Genesis.) Keith was looking to see if he could acquire yet another bass to add to his collection before setting off to sound check for the final gig.

No gig is the same – the venue, the audience, everything feeds off everything else. You get one kind of energy coming off the stage, another coming from the crowd and as a photographer you feed off this, trying to capture it. The music reverberates round in your head, at once deafening and distant. Although surrounded by thousands of people you feel isolated, cocooned in the sound, looking for patterns, always trying to simplify, to find the essence of the mood and the atmosphere. Shooting a concert in colour is quite different to shooting in black and white. It adds a whole new dimension because with the sweeping light-show, the colour is constantly changing. The colour gives a sense of excitement, pulling you into the fantasy.

The last gig of the tour over, it was time for farewells. It was half past one before we got to bed. Though not for long. At half past five next morning we set off for the location of the video shoot. The guys were all knackered and there wasn't much said in between naps on the hour-long drive out into the countryside. As usual when on the move I sat bang awake, enjoying the sun rising as we sped through a new land.

The video was being directed by Nigel Dick and shot by Russell Swanson who had already worked with The Corrs on their 'Only When I Sleep' video in LA. It looked like the weather would

hold out and spirits were as high as they could be at that hour of the morning before breakfast.

After a good start it began to rain and there was nothing to do but wait it out. The band retreated to the caravan that served as a dressing room and within minutes they were all asleep. It was ironic to have come halfway around the world to shoot a video in a place that looked like home only to fall foul of some typically Irish weather.

Working on a film set is a pretty boring affair for all those involved, requiring an immense

Half past five in the morning and the band wait to go to the location of the video shoot and breakfast.

Director and cinematographer discuss
shots as the band are made ready
for the video. A group of primary
schoolkids stumble across the
shoot on their way home.

amount of patience. For passers-by it has all the fascination of a crossword puzzle. Even out here on a little back road we gathered ourselves an audience. A group of primary school kids on their way home found their path blocked by the filming. They sat happily watching until the way was clear and they could leave with their heads full of pop stars and films.

As the sun set the director squeezed the last shots out of the day and it was off to the car and back to the hotel. The Corrs, who only had a couple of hours to shower and change before their flight home, went straight to their rooms. I had the luxury of a good six or seven hours sleep. On the other hand I was flying economy; they were going first class. But as John pointed out, they'd aged years in economy.

How it all finally looked.

dreams

Back home in Ireland I set about finding a publisher in the UK. I felt I had a great set of pictures and a unique angle on a band that was taking the world by storm. Once again the business studies text books were pulled down from the shelf. I put together an illustrated proposal and backed it up with a detailed breakdown on the band's three million sales worldwide.

To my astonishment I wasn't immediately overwhelmed by offers. In spite of their appeal in Australasia and parts of Europe, and their almost miraculous success in Ireland, both north and south of the border, The Corrs were still practically unknown in mainland Britain. No matter what they did – live performances, press interviews – no one would give them the airplay they needed. It seemed that if you weren't on the Radio One or Capital Radio play list, you didn't exist.

In the early days John Hughes had used all his skills to get a record deal. Now he put his mind to conquering the UK. The only way to counter radio's bolted door, he decided, was mainstream television exposure. A radical plan was required and a radical plan was what he got. John Giddings, the band's UK agent, suggested hiring the Albert Hall in advance of The Corrs' British tour and persuading the BBC to televise it live. And there was only one day that would do: 17 March 1998, St Patrick's Day.

The idea of playing the Albert Hall was scary. Not just because it came with so much history, but because it was huge and what if no one turned up? The fan base in Britain was an unknown quantity. Surely there could be nothing worse than pictures of a half-empty auditorium going out live?

A trump in their hand was that Mick Fleetwood had agreed to make a guest appearance. The

This simple shot of Sharon at The Point, Dublin was much harder to get than it looks.

Mick Fleetwood, the BBC, the Albert Hall and St Patrick's Day all play their part in helping to turn the tide for the band in the UK.

band had recently recorded their version of Fleetwood Mac's classic rock ballad 'Dreams' for the album of Fleetwood Mac covers, *Rumours Revisited*. 'Dreams' had been released as the album's single.

The plan itself worked like a dream and the BBC were soon safely on board. I arranged to go to London to cover what I sensed would be a key moment in the band's history. That was the plan, anyway. I arrived at the Albert Hall to find that the BBC had prohibited all access, either before or after the show. It was the dreaded 'first three songs' or nothing. I found John who, though more than a little preoccupied, said that he'd see what he could do. Nothing happened. Finally he said that the only person who might be able to swing something was Lee Ellen who handled The Corrs' PR in the UK and who would be back later.

I had no alternative but to wait and settled down to watch the sound check. I recognized some of the signs of nervousness in the band. They were all rather subdued, trying to focus on their set as a rake of cameramen whirled and zipped around them. The arrival of Mick Fleetwood lightened the proceedings. Although they had often cited him in press interviews as one of their heroes, there was no obvious change of demeanour. They always enjoyed the company of other musicians, but they were never in awe, just glad of the distraction.

That night, in the side lobby of the hall, were close to twenty photographers. Because there were so many it was decided that we would be processed in groups of six, each group getting three songs. As we waited I heard someone mention Lee Ellen's name. I went up and introduced myself, told her about the book and of my problem. She recognized my name and asked if I had taken a certain Christmas shot of the band. I nodded as she said that she loved it and that it was her favourite photo of The Corrs and she would see what she could do. As good as her word she returned fifteen minutes later to say I could stay for the entire show as long as I kept a low profile. I'd had plenty of practice of that in Sydney.

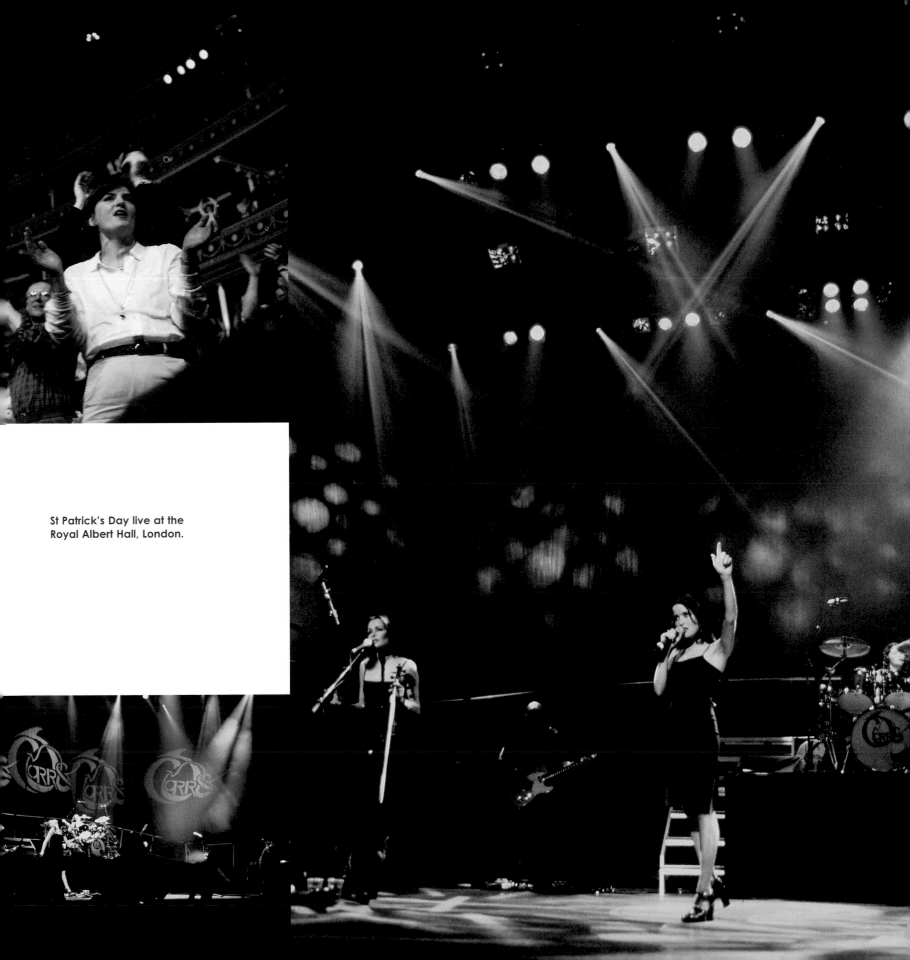

St Patrick's Day live at the
Royal Albert Hall, London.

The show was just starting as we were led in. The place was packed with all seats taken. Being St Patrick's Day there was a large Irish contingent. The press was being wooed and it was junket city for those from the record industry.

It wasn't exactly make or break time for the band but if this didn't put them on the UK map, ideas were pretty thin on the ground. It all nearly went horribly wrong. At a few minutes past eleven the lonely strains of

Sharon's violin created the required hush in the auditorium. But on television screens around the country a caption appeared reading 'We're sorry for the interference on sound'. What sound? There was no sound. Three whole minutes of no sound. More than enough time to switch channels or switch off. It looked like a cruel quirk of fate was about to deny The Corrs this chance to show the British public what they did and who they were.

Back in the auditorium the arrival of Mick Fleetwood on stage added to the excitement, an excitement that the band sustained up to the end of the performance. As they took their by now trademark final bow they were all visibly moved by the reaction of the crowd. Andrea was close to tears.

The music business is a lottery. Nobody knows what will be popular and the record companies sign and drop more bands than ever reach the top. It seemed that in spite of the three minutes silence, the British public hadn't turned off. Within a week *Talk On Corners* went straight to number thirteen and has stayed in the Top Twenty ever since, going to number one on six separate occasions. The UK is a big prize in the music business pot. It is big enough, with a large enough media, to be self-regarding and it can seem that if you're big in Britain you're big all over the world. After the Albert Hall The Corrs had a ticket for this prize. And I had an offer on the book.

By the time the autumn tour of Britain came around the band was one of the hottest acts in the country. The tour was a sell out, including five Wembley Arena dates. If the Arena hadn't been booked out they would have played a longer run – as it was they had to move their sixth London gig to Docklands.

John and his wife, Marie,
enjoy the splendour of success back at the
hotel after the end of show party following the
band's opening Wembly Arena gig.

I joined them for the first London show, meeting up in the lobby of the hotel before we headed for the tour bus that would take us on the hour's ride to Wembley. Outside the hotel a small group of fans were waiting. They chatted with the band for a while before handing them some letters and a present or two. Once on the bus – a real upstairs, downstairs affair – Andrea wondered aloud how on earth they had found them. The band changes hotels regularly so as to avoid huge numbers of fans hanging about but somehow a few always discover where they are. They recognized this group of enthusiasts from other gigs; in fact, they told the band that they had

been to every gig on the tour.

Andrea set about reading the letters while Sharon told everyone about her conversation with three of the fans. They'd said that they loved her violin playing but that they hated one particular melody line. She waited expectantly for her siblings' comments. They weren't slow in coming. They'd never really liked it either, they said. Then Sharon admitted ruefully that she'd had her doubts herself but she couldn't believe that no one else had ever mentioned it. She changed it that night.

At Wembley I had to keep
my distance as the band
were nervous at the prospect
of stepping up a league in
the UK.

Andrea looked up from the letter she was reading. 'This letter is so sweet,' she said. 'They say that they want to meet up for a girls' night out, just as friends. How can we? They'd never be able to see us as anything but The Corrs.'

Also on the bus that night were their parents, Jean and Gerry Corr, who come to the gigs whenever they can. It must be amazing to watch your children enjoy and excel at something you yourself love and that you yourself taught them. When they're around the atmosphere becomes more domestic and it's strange to hear the band refer to them as 'mammy' and 'daddy'.

Such was The Corrs' popularity that they were in constant demand. The Albert Hall concert had been a watershed. If they had thought they were in the spotlight before, they were now finding out what stardom was really like. With Wembley they had stepped up to the premier division in the UK and were very nervous. I was asked to give them a wide berth before the show so they could relax as much as possible, which I was very happy to do.

You have to give people space and you can't take pictures of everything. You just get what you get. A lot of it is just looking and being prepared for what happens. The more you watch people, the more you see how they act and react, and then you capture it. One of the things about taking photographs is that it isolates you from everyone else, because you're constantly watching. You try not to freak people out, but they know you're watching them all the time.

The band went down a storm and were on an obvious high after the show. Celebrities were beginning to turn up at the gigs and backstage. The Corrs were the hottest thing around.

That night the record company threw a big bash for them in a club in central London. The club was large and full and as the band came in a spontaneous round of applause broke out. You could see that they were both flattered and a bit embarrassed by their reception, smiling shyly and rather self-consciously as they were led through to the VIP area. It was already half full. As John sat down he realized that he didn't recognize anyone and he started going through the interlopers one by one asking, 'Who are you?', before getting them to leave the table.

The Christmas break came with the news that *Talk On Corners* had turned out to be 1998's biggest UK seller. It would go on to win a Brit award along with other awards in countries such as Spain and Ireland. Even the crew picked up an award for their professionalism. The break wasn't to be a time for reflection, however, as The Corrs were already gearing up for two gigs at Dublin's Point Theatre before heading off on the second leg of their British tour.

The pressure had come to a head. The UK success had been so phenomenal and sudden that they were over-committed, with things they had agreed to do before the whirlwind clashing with things they really needed to do now if they weren't to lose their momentum.

It was into this atmosphere that I entered The Point. The band were by now rapidly tiring of the constant attention. Whereas once they actively sought interviews and media coverage, now

the tables were turned. Everyone wanted them. All they wanted was to be left alone. And that included me.

They had been on the go for a full eighteen months since completing the album and they really wanted some time off. They had a month pencilled in around April but it was now only January and they were about to head off to the States to tour and promote. Who knew what could happen between now and then?

I could hear that a sound check was in progress and so I headed for the stage. From the look on their faces I could tell that they weren't expecting me but I took a few shots as they finished up. They were tired. They didn't understand why I wanted to go to another concert and take more photographs. Hadn't I got enough? But from a visual perspective the show had changed radically, throwing up a whole new raft of images. And even though I knew my presence wasn't entirely welcome, I had to stand my ground. My job, as I saw it, was to chart the progression, like snapshots in time. I didn't know what was going to change. I didn't know what was going to happen. And that was part of what drove me on.

At The Point the band's sound
had gone up another level.

Even though I couldn't get too close the new screens gave me another dimension to shoot.

As at Wembley, there were the new giant video screens so that you wouldn't miss a nuance and these were accompanied by editing and camera crews. The sound once again was bigger and more powerful, while The Corrs were each more assured of their ability to take their turn in the limelight, Jim on piano, Sharon and Caroline doing a duet. By the second night they were more confident still and with the encouragement of another showman they ordered the crowd to get up and dance. 'They're just waiting for you to tell them.' He was right.

I was going around trying to capture the mood. On the first night I hadn't even entered the pit in front of stage but on this night I went in about halfway through the set. I was trying to get something new, maybe by using the screens in some way, but it wasn't long before I was asked to leave and so had to go back to shooting from further away. John said, 'It's nothing personal, they're just sick of cameras. If you were anyone else you wouldn't be here, we wouldn't even be having this conversation.'

They left for the UK the next day with the news that their Lansdowne Road gig was not only going ahead but that it had sold twenty thousand tickets in the first week.

It's amazing how the colour of the lighting can affect the mood. The blue in this case gives a calm, intimate feel to the performance.

touchdown

The book was nearly done, photographs honed and re-honed, design agreed, text in the final stage of completion. Now there was only the finale of the Lansdowne Road stadium concert for me to cover. The increasing distance I'd experienced over the past year had left me unsure of whether I was going to get the access I needed.

The band had been away a lot, touring in Europe, Australasia, South East Asia, and in the States with the Rolling Stones. They'd also found much needed time off. I hadn't seen them for over six months. Although I had more than enough material for the book, I also knew that the Lansdowne Road gig in front of a home crowd of over 42,000 would give it symmetry and a natural climax.

I had spent quite a bit of time working with John on the book but with the concert barely a week away, I still didn't know whether I was going to cover it or not. I had prepared myself with a range of arguments but John in his usual unexpected way side-stepped me with, 'No? I want you to cover it.' And that was that.

Now there only remained the problem of doing a good job. Instead of having the luxury of a whole tour, or a series of gigs as at Wembley, I'd only have two hours. Also there was the small point that I'd never covered a stadium gig before.

It takes a good week to get everything in place. The crew was already practised, having done one stadium gig in Nottingham to a capacity audience of 35,000 a few weeks before. By the time I arrived the stadium was in the calm before the storm. In one of the old clubrooms at the corner of the

Andrea and Caroline watch the unfolding of the intro video for their Lansdowne Road concert.

pitch a production meeting had been called. The final decisions were being made as to the stage's positioning, sound and light requirements and the positioning of the rake of cameras that would document the occasion. The whole affair was very informal with people coming and going as needs be. Later on I heard someone ask, 'When is the production meeting?' The reply came, 'That was it.'

It soon became apparent that nothing very photographic was going to happen and after getting the kind of backroom dealing shots that I wanted and some shots of this huge empty space, I headed off.

A couple of days later I arrived for the press call. Everything was being set up, transforming a rugby pitch into a vast open-air theatre. Every square inch of turf was being overlaid by rectangles of thick plastic flooring, which also served to cover the jumble of cables.

I climbed all around the stadium, getting a feel for it, to see what would make a good vantage point, to try to save some time during the event itself. I ran off some shots of the preparations. More than anywhere else, I felt what I needed to do here was to capture the event, the scale, the sheer volume of people. I also discovered that one of my lenses had a minor problem. Better to find out now than after the show itself. After about an hour it was time to check out the press call.

At the production meeting John runs through the organizational details for the concert.

One-to-one interviews were now largely a thing of the past. The band were led out to the awaiting forty or fifty journalists who asked a range of not very original questions and received a range of not very original answers.

Next it was the photo call where about twenty photographers took a series of shots of the band posing on stage, in front of the stage and throwing a rugby ball in the air. I stood back and watched as photographers jostled for position. As the stage was still being constructed they all had to wear hard hats. The band, of course, were bareheaded. So if anything fell the photographers would be all right but the band would be dead.

Saturday was showtime. I waved my hellos and started working shortly before 1 p.m. when the band was already sound checking. The number of people around them was amazing. Scattered across the stadium were sixteen camera crews. On stage and immediately in front of the stage were five cameras, one on a crane, two on stands, one on stage and one on a dolly. Four more handheld cameras recorded every move the band made. I stayed back until John told me it was okay to go up on stage but to be careful to stay out of the band's eye lines and not to overstay my welcome.

The band sound check and the camera and production crews get ready for the night's show, stopping only to allow the Gardaí to carry out a bomb search.

Although many of the original crew who remembered me from Ireland and Australia were still on the team, they were outnumbered by dozens of others who had no idea who I was. The previous day the security guard wouldn't even let me in until I dropped half a dozen of the right names. For the night itself, everyone involved in the show was given a laminate. All laminates are graded. Grade One lets you into the dressing rooms backstage. Grade Two gets you in everywhere else. I was Grade Two. But that night I wandered around the stadium and didn't even try to get backstage. What was important to me was the scale of things outside and I already had thousands of shots of the band backstage. Ironically, at one point they were looking for me to take a photo but couldn't find me.

This was the first time that the band and John saw the intro video. The video set up the necessary excitement in the crowd for the band's entrance.

About half an hour before the show I was sitting in catering having a coffee and giving my gear a last-minute check. John happened by and asked me what I would need during the show. I told him I needed to be on stage when they came on and I needed to be on stage for the encore. He went off to suss it out with the guys, coming back a little later to say that it was fine, just to stay on the side of the stage and keep out of the way. Everyone was naturally a bit tense.

At about ten to nine I took up my position. The tenseness extended to the crew and cameramen here too. It seemed that everyone had some last-minute task to do that was really annoying someone else. In the cramped conditions people were bumping each other and, more aggravatingly, each other's equipment as they rectified their own problems. Cameramen were checking positioning, light readings and cables, the crew were trying to keep everything clear as they checked instruments and radio mikes, while the riggers were climbing all over the set, up and down tiny rope ladders, to the cheers and jeers of the crowd.

I did my best to stay out of all this while still maintaining my good vantage point. I was quite worried about the lighting. It was still daylight but dusk would soon be upon us. Also, I hadn't expected the huge black curtain that had been drawn across the stage, making it much darker than out front. Furthermore, when it was pulled back and the lights were switched on the whole situation was going to change dramatically. I swapped the film in my cameras twice before I decided to stop fretting and relax, telling myself that I was as prepared as I was ever going to be.

Keith and Anto came on stage first, closely followed by the band. They all went around wishing each other luck before taking up their positions. The roar of the crowd could be heard as the intro music thumped out. There was an eerie calm on stage as everyone waited. Jim watched the big screen behind Caroline on which the accompanying intro video was rolling. I hoped that Andrea and Sharon weren't as terrified as they looked. The intro ended, the curtains opened and there was a rush of energy from the crowd. All I remember seeing was people, thousands of mad people.

After the rapturous opening I left the stage and went down to the pit, which was well named. The stage is thirty feet up and you fight for space with photographers and camera crews. Unwanted heads and arms ruined some shots while there was one cameraman who zoomed back and forward on the dolly tracks and seemed to pop into frame at just the right moment.

From the pit I moved around the stadium to try to use all the vantage points I'd scouted previously. As I pushed through the crowd I did feel quite jealous of the camera crew with their

stations all over the stadium, covering everything from a myriad of angles, giving them the luxury of mountains of material to edit later. I, on the other hand, had to shoot everything myself, lugging my gear around and hoping I wasn't missing anything too important as I trudged up the flights of stairs to the top of the stand. I'd learned years ago that you couldn't shoot everything, that there were always going to be times when you weren't there or when your camera simply ran out of film.

The gig shot from different angles.
To be involved in something that
so many people attended was amazing.

As I went through the crowd it seemed that everyone wanted their photo taken. They all wanted to know what paper it was for and they were all convinced that since I wasn't using a flash I hadn't taken their picture. I battled on.

After another brief spell in the pit I headed back on stage for the encore. As the finale approached I was making my way to the stage entrance, only to be stopped by a security guard. 'Nobody can come through here,' he said. 'But I'm going on stage,' I replied. 'I'm sorry but you'll have to go around,' he insisted, meaning that I'd have to go out into the crowd, come back in through another entrance and pass two feet behind him to get on the stage. Naturally I wasn't impressed. Just then he said the same thing to two other guys who were trying to get through. 'They won't let us out that way either,' they replied. I was getting less impressed by the minute. I

remonstrated with the guard, showed him my Access All Areas laminate, but he was adamant. There was nothing he could do until his boss came back.

At that moment a guy carrying a film camera magazine tried to get past. 'It's okay, I'm working,' he said, shortly followed by the squeal, 'but I'm making a documentary,' as he tried to push his way through. I was about to use this distraction to make a break for it when the sheriff arrived in the shape of the head of security and waved us all through.

Back on stage the tension had been ratcheted up a notch, side-stage at least. There were so many cameramen trying to get shots that it was difficult to find a spot to stand in. I always try to give the other guys their space but sometimes they are not so charitable. I was lining up a shot of Jim working the crowd when one of the cameramen simply jumped in front of me. My blood

The crowd were roaring and screaming. Andrea was so knocked out that she just started screaming back at them.

boiled and I seriously considered giving him a kick. Instead I decided to try my luck on the other side of the stage.

From here I could see John and the look on his face was priceless. There was a time when he was so nervous that he could barely bring himself to watch the band's performances. Gradually he progressed to watching some and then more of the shows, most times arms folded and distant, sometimes even with a quiet smile. Now as the band were running through the final song of the encore he was bouncing up and down in time to the music.

The encore finished, the floodlight came on, the crowd roared and my cameras ran out of film. The band came off stage, joined John and headed off under the stand and out of the stadium. Game over.

acknowledgements

I'd like to thank Andrea, Caroline, Jim and Sharon for allowing me the opportunity of doing this book. I'd especially like to thank John Hughes without whom this all would simply not have happened. I'd also like to say a word of thanks to Henry McGrogan, Anto Drennan, Keith Duffy, Emma Hill and the rest of The Corrs' crew for putting up with me over the years.

I'd like to express my gratitude to my mum, my dad and to Mark and Una for all their help and support and for that matter to my Aunt Anne and my Gran.

I'd like to thank Ingrid Connell for all her help and patience, Pepsy Dening for her work on the project and Stella Wilkins and everybody at Abner Stein. Also thanks to Colm Murray and Dermot Quinn at CMB Design for their help and support and to Steve Averill and Siobhan at ABA for their advice. I'd also like to give a mention to Jim, Paddy and Eamon at Repro 35 and Niall and Dave at ISS for their help, their advice and most of all their enlightened credit policies.

There are also innumerable people to whom I owe a debt of gratitude, some of whom I'm bound to forget as I type this out at the last minute but here goes. Thanks to Jonathan and Jane, to Bryan, to Terrie, Brian, Connor, Sharon, Ciara, Simon, Anne and Colin and the rest of the amoeba, to Brendan, Deirdre, Lal, Michel, Dell, Alex, Ashling, Hugh, Ronnie, to Geoff, Hanan, Jane, Cliona, Simon and Fintan, to John Giddings, Andy Murray, Lee Ellen, Michael Scott and Nick Pedgritt and to Dennis Desmond, Daryl Downey and all at MCD.